Written by Megan Faulkner

Designed by Bill Henderson and Leanne Thomas

Scholastic and Tangerine Press and associated logos are trademarks of Scholastic Inc.

Published by Tangerine Press, an imprint of Scholastic Inc., 557 Broadway, New York, NY 10012

10 9 8 7 6 5 4 3 2 1
ISBN: 978-0-545-73452-3

Printed and bound in Guangzhou, China

Photo Credits

Photographs ©: iStockphoto/Baxternator: box sides geode, iStockphoto: 2 top left, 2 bottom right (agcuesta), 5 top, 23 top (Andreyuu), 6 top (Baxternator), 7 top (Beboy_ltd), 11 top (BooostedAWD), 23 bottom right (Bryngelzon), 7 bottom (chrisbradshaw), 19 (Difydave), 20 top (FokinOl), 28 (grahambedingfield), 22 (gremlin), 2 top right, 2 center, 2 bottom left, 8, 20 bottom, 21 (hsvrs), 6 bottom left, 18 (ivansmuk), 6 bottom right (jdwfoto), 14 (Jodi Jacobson), 4 (Karol Kozlowski), 5 bottom, 16 top (KatarzynaBialasiewicz), 15 bottom (kyoshino), 23 bottom left (mikeuk), 16 bottom (pryzmat), 18 inset (Renewer), 25 (Rob_Ellis), 17, 24 (SunChan), 15 top, 30 (Terry Wilson), 3 (valeaielli), 10, 11 bottom (worakit), 9 (zanskar); Leanne Thomas: 4 inset; Tangerine Press Photo: cover images, 1 and background throughout, 12 bottom left & right, 13 bottom, 13 top.

TABLE OF CONTENTS

WELCOME, ROCK STARS!

Whether you are an experienced rockhound or a fledgling Rockpup, breaking open a geode is always exciting. The crystal treasure inside is millions of years old, and YOU are the first human to lay eyes on it.

IN YOUR KIT

This kit will unlock and help you understand the mysterious world of geodes.

HERE'S WHAT YOU GET

- Geodes—to open and examine
- Safety glasses—to protect your eyes from rock dust and splinters
- A magnifying glass—to study your geodes closely

YOU'LL ALSO NEED

- Hammer
- Flathead screwdriver
- Pencil
- Paper
- Ruler
- Camera (optional)
- 3 large eggs
- Alum powder (potassium aluminum sulfate)
- Food coloring
- White glue
- Paintbrush
- 6 glasses or jars
- Pushpin
- Small pair of pointed scissors
- Old sock that can be thrown away

WARNING

- ONLY INTENDED FOR PEOPLE 8 YEARS UP! AN ADULT HELPER IS REQUIRED!
- UNDERSTAND ALL OF THE SAFETY INSTRUCTIONS BEFORE STARTING.
- ALWAYS ASK AN ADULT TO HELP YOU WITH THE TOOLS THAT YOU NEED.
- NEVER BORROW TOOLS WITHOUT ASKING. IT IS NOT ONLY RUDE, BUT DANGEROUS.
- BE MINDFUL OF PEOPLE AND ANIMALS WHEN YOU CRACK OPEN YOUR GEODE.
- ALWAYS WEAR YOUR SAFETY GOGGLES WHEN WORKING ON THE GEODE.
- BE CERTAIN THAT YOU FIND A SAFE AND WEL-VENTILATED AREA.
- NEVER BREAK OPEN THE GEODE INSIDE YOUR HOUSE. PIECES CAN FLY AND BREAK THINGS.
- NEVER BREAK OPEN THE GEODE ON A FINISHED SURFACE, LIKE A FLOOR OR CARPET.
- NEVER HOLD THE GEODE WHEN HAMMERING.
- ROCK PIECES MAY FLY OUT AND INJURE YOU OR OTHERS. BE CAREFUL.
- DO NOT INHALE ANY OF THE GEODE DUST.
- ALWAYS CLEAN UP ANY LEFTOVER PIECES AND DISPOSE OF THEM SAFELY.

GEODES 101

A geode is a hollow cavity in **igneous** or **sedimentary** rock that is lined with inward-facing mineral crystals. The mineral layers develop slowly from a hard cryptocrystalline outer shell. It takes millions of years for a geode to form. They range in size from inches to feet.

While it's true that most geodes are spherical, rectangles, triangles, and other shapes are sometimes found.

DID YOU KNOW? The word *geode* comes from the Greek word for "earthlike."

HOW A GEODE IS FORMED

Geodes develop in the spaces left by gas bubbles in igneous rock, and in holes from animal burrows and tree roots in sedimentary rock. Water trickles into the empty space and leaves minerals behind. Layers of crystallized minerals slowly build inward from a hard outer shell. Over time, the softer rock around the cavity erodes and the geode is left at ground level, waiting to be discovered.

Geodes are found around the world but are mostly found in the United States, Brazil, and Namibia. Within the United States, California, Arizona, Utah, Nevada, Illinois, Missouri, Kentucky, and Iowa have large deposits due to expansive outcroppings of the volcanic rock **rhyolite**. Rhyolite lava is extra gassy, which means more bubbles to harden into geode-friendly cavities. Vast former lake beds of sedimentary rock are also conducive to geode formation.

EXPERIMENT
CAN YOU JUDGE A GEODE BY ITS COVER?

We're so used to seeing rocks in our environment, it's easy to overlook their individual characteristics. A successful rockhound needs strong visual and mental focus. Try the following experiment to sharpen your powers of observation.

RESEARCH QUESTION

From the outside, an unopened geode looks like an ordinary rock. Are there any external characteristics on your geodes that might predict what's inside? Write down your ideas.

_____

_____

_____

_____

_____

_____

_____

_____

HERE'S WHAT YOU'LL NEED

- Geodes
- Pencil or camera
- Paper
- Ruler

PROCEDURE

1. Photograph or sketch your unopened geodes.
2. Write a description of the exterior of each geode. Include information about its size, shape, and color.
3. Make a prediction about what you think you will find inside the geode.
4. With the help of an adult, open your geodes one at a time using one of the methods on page 10-12.
5. Take a picture or sketch the inside of each geode. Write a description of each interior, including information about its size, shape, and color.

OBSERVATIONS

Compare the actual descriptions with your predictions. What predictions were correct? What observations surprised you?

CONCLUSION

Analyze the data and draw a conclusion. Does the outside of a geode predict what is on the inside?

DID YOU KNOW?

You know the old saying "You can't judge a book by its cover"? Well, you can't judge a geode

OPENING YOUR GEODE

It's time for the big reveal! You've studied the outside of your geodes and made notes and predictions. Now comes the fun part — finding out what's inside! Choose one of the methods below and get crackin'!

METHOD NO. 1

This is the safest way to open a geode, but there is no way to control how many pieces the geode will break into.

YOU'LL NEED THE TOOLS FROM THIS KIT, A HAMMER, AND AN OLD SOCK THAT CAN BE THROWN AWAY WHEN YOU'RE DONE.

DID YOU KNOW ?

If you want to split the geode into two equal halves, use Method No. 2.

1. Find a hard surface to work on, such as a cement floor or a sidewalk or driveway.
2. Put one geode inside the sock and lay it on the ground.
3. Put on your safety glasses.
4. Hit the geode with a hammer until it cracks open.
5. Repeat with the remaining geodes.

Warning:
Don't Forget!

When all the geodes have been opened, throw away the safety sock, because it will have tiny, sharp splinters of rock inside.

M THOD NO. 2

It will take a little longer to open your geodes using this method, but you'll have more control over how they break apart.

YOU'LL NEED THE TOOLS FROM YOUR KIT, PLUS A HAMMER AND FLATHEAD SCREWDRIVER.

1. Decide if you want to open your geode lengthwise or widthwise.
2. Put on your safety glasses.
3. Use the flathead screwdriver to lightly score (leave an indented trail) around the geode where you want it to break.
4. Keep scoring until you see a little crack.
5. Hold the flathead screwdriver lightly over the crack, and gently tap the end with your hammer.
6. Keep gently tapping until the geode breaks open.

WHAT YOU MIGHT FIND IN YOUR GEODES

Opening a geode is the easy part. Identifying what's inside can be challenging. The following chapters will help you learn some tricks of the trade.

QUARTZ:
A GEODE'S BEST FRIEND

When you open a geode, you might find quartz crystals inside. Quartz is a combination of silicon dioxide and oxygen. It is one of the most abundant minerals on Earth. And it comes in a ton of varieties and colors.

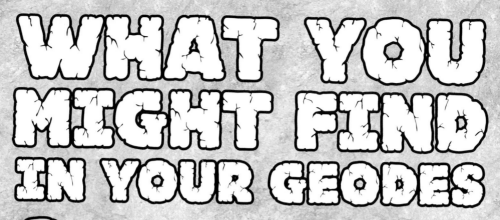

CLEAR QUARTZ

Also called rock quartz, pure quartz, and ice quartz, clear quartz is colorless and transparent. Until the seventeenth century, clear quartz was believed to be ice that was so frozen it would never thaw.

MILKY QUARTZ

The most frequently occurring quartz color, an opaque, milky finish results from gases and/or liquids trapped during crystallization. Milky quartz is not desirable for use in jewelry because of its opacity.

Opacity is the quality of a material that does not allow light to pass through it.

DID YOU KNOW?

SMOKY QUARTZ

A gray, translucent quartz. It ranges in clarity from almost completely transparent to a nearly opaque brownish-gray. Some can even be black.

AMETHYST

Amethyst is classified as a semiprecious gemstone and is often used in jewelry. The translucent crystals range from a vivid purple to a dull violet. The color is a result of iron impurities.

Amethyst is said to calm the mind, protect from negative people and situations, and increase determination.

CITRINE

This pale yellow to brown quartz is primarily found in Brazil. Natural citrine is very rare. Most of the citrine available for purchase is actually heat-treated amethyst that turns yellow when exposed to high temperatures.

CHALCEDONY

This cryptocrystalline variant of quartz includes a small amount of moganite. Cryptocrystalline means the individual crystals are so tiny that they cannot even be viewed under a microscope unless the sample is shaved so thinly that light can shine through it.
When chalcedony grows in concentric layers it is called agate.

Chalcedony is thought to increase creativity and artistic expression. It is the stone of friendship and goodwill.

OTHER MINERALS THAT CAN BE FOUND IN GEODES ARE CALCITE, PYRITE, KAOLINITE, SPHALERITE, MILLERITE, **BARITE**, **DOLOMITE**, LIMONITE, AND SMITHSONITE.

GEODE SPECIALISTS

Every rock and mineral tells a story about the history of our planet—you just need to learn the language.

Geology is the scientific study of the origin, history, and structure of the earth. A geologist is a scientist who works in this field. Rocks are their textbooks. The work of geologists affects our lives every day: from mining and the management of natural resources to education and warnings about natural hazards like earthquakes, tsunamis, and volcanoes.

Geologists who focus on the distribution, identification, and properties of minerals are called mineralogists.

Geologists who concentrate on crystal structure are called crystallographers. They study geodes, too!

THE PHYSICAL PROPERTIES OF MINERALS

Minerals are identified by the following physical properties:

COLOR

Opaque minerals are quite consistent in color, but the color of translucent to transparent minerals is easily changed by the presence of trace impurities. Thus, color alone is not recommended as a method of identification.

STREAK

Streak is the color of the powder a mineral leaves when it is scratched across a special plate. Sometimes the streak is a different color from the mineral itself. For instance, hematite can be silver or red but its streak is always red.

TRANSPARENCY

Transparency refers to how well light passes through a mineral sample. There are three degrees of transparency: transparent, translucent, and opaque.

- You can see objects through a transparent mineral.
- You can see light but no objects through a translucent mineral.
- You can't see anything through an opaque mineral.

LUSTER

Luster is the way the surface of a mineral reflects light. There are two types of luster: metallic and nonmetallic. The terms used to describe luster are:

Metallic	**Example:** gold
Vitreous (glassy)	**Example:** quartz, tourmaline
Adamantine (brilliant)	**Example:** diamond
Greasy or **waxy**	**Example:** turquoise
Pearly	**Example:** talc
Silky	**Example:** asbestos
Dull or earthy	**Example:** bauxite
Resinous (like resin or sap from a tree)	**Example:** amber

CLEAVAGE

When a mineral sample is broken with a hammer, it breaks along planes of weakness that are part of its crystalline structure. These breaks are cleavages. Some minerals break only in one direction. Others break in two or more directions.

- Cubic cleavages form cubes (example: halite).
- Rhombohedral cleavages form six-sided prisms (example: calcite).
- Basal cleavages occur along a single plane parallel to the base of the mineral (example: topaz).

DID YOU KNOW?

If a mineral breaks easily and cleanly in one or more directions, its cleavage is considered perfect.

HARDNESS

Hardness is the measure of how easily a mineral can be scratched. The Mohs' scale ranks ten well-known minerals from one to ten. One is the softest and ten is the hardest.

MOHS' HARDNESS SCALE									
1	2	3	4	5	6	7	8	9	10
Talc	Gypsum	Calcite	Fluorite	Apatite	Feldspar	Quartz	Topaz	Corundum	Diamond

FRACTURE

Some minerals fracture in a smoothly curved, irregular, jagged, or splintery manner instead of the clean, flat break of a cleavage. The most common fractures are conchoidal (quartz), fibrous or splintery, hackly (copper), and uneven or irregular.

SPECIFIC GRAVITY (SG)

Specific gravity is the density of a mineral. With a little practice, you can guess a mineral's SG by hand. Some mineral samples will feel heavier than others, even similarly sized samples. The heavier ones have a greater SG. Here are some examples of common minerals and their SG ranges:

MINERALS	DENSITY	SPECIFIC GRAVITY
sulfur, graphite	light	1-2
gypsum, quartz	medium	2-3
fluorite, beryl	medium heavy	3-4
corundum, most metal oxides	heavy	4-6
native gold	heavier	19
platinum	heaviest	21+

CRYSTAL FORM

Minerals usually crystallize into one of six crystal systems defined by the axes of the crystal, the angles at which the axes intersect, and the degree of symmetry.

Isometric Also called the cubic crystal system. Crystals are usually shaped like blocks, with similar and symmetrical faces. The crystal has three axes of symmetry, all at right angles to each other, and all of the same length.
Example: pyrite

Tetragonal Typically, the crystals are shaped like four-sided prisms and pyramids. Each crystal has three axes, all perpendicular to one another. Two axes are the same length and lie on a horizontal plane. The third axis is not the same length and is at a right angle to the other two.
Example: zircon

Hexagonal These crystals are usually shaped like six-sided prisms or pyramids. Each crystal has four axes of symmetry. Three lie in the same plane, are the same length, and intersect at 120-degree angles. The fourth axis is not the same length, and is perpendicular to the other three.
Example: beryl

Orthorhombic These crystals are short and stubby. Each crystal has three unequal axes, all at right angles to one another.
Example: topaz

Monoclinic Crystals are short and stubby with tilted faces at each end. Each crystal has three unequal axes. Two axes lie in the same plane at right angles to each other. The third axis is inclined.
Example: gypsum

Triclinic Crystals are usually flat with sharp edges, but exhibit no right angles. Each crystal has three unequal axes. None are perpendicular to one another.
Example: feldspar

EXPERIMENT
MAKE YOUR OWN
EGG GEODES

Geodes take millions of years to develop, but you can make one in only a few days!

YOU WILL NEED

- 3 large eggs
- Alum powder (potassium aluminum sulfate)
- Food coloring
- White glue
- Paintbrush
- 6 glasses or jars
- Pushpin
- Small pair of pointed scissors

Alum powder can be found in the spice section of your local grocery store. If they don't carry it, you can order it online.

DID YOU KNOW?

INSTRUCTIONS

DAY 1

1. Carefully make a hole in each end of the egg with a pushpin.
2. Over a bowl, bring one end of the egg to your lips and gently blow the yolk out the other end.
3. Insert your scissors into one of the holes and cut the egg in half lengthwise.
4. Use some soapy water to gently wash the inside of the shells. Pat the egg dry with a paper towel and wash your hands well.
5. When the shells are completely dry, put a small squirt of white glue on the inside of each shell. Use the paintbrush to completely coat the inside surface.
6. Generously sprinkle alum powder all over the glued area.
7. Let the shells dry overnight.

DAY 2

8. Stir ¾ cup (177 ml) of alum into 2 cups (473 ml) of very hot water until the alum crystals dissolve completely.
   Tip: If the hot water from the faucet doesn't do the trick, pop the solution in the microwave for a minute at a time until the alum dissolves.
9. Use a separate jar for each color. Mason jars work great. Pour an equal amount of water into each jar.
10. Add 20-30 drops of food coloring to each jar. Follow the directions on the food-coloring package to achieve the colors you want. Stir each mixture with a spoon.
11. Let the jars cool for 30 minutes. Gently place one eggshell in each jar. Make sure the shell is completely covered by the mixture.
12. Do not touch your eggshells for a minimum of 12 hours. Then carefully remove the shells to check the size of the crystals. The longer you leave the shells in the jar, the bigger the crystals will grow.

GEODE TRIVIA & FOLKLORE

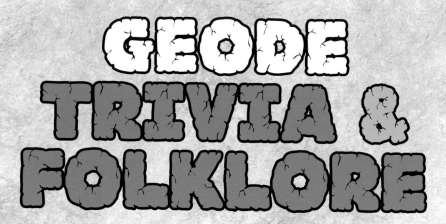

- In the United Kingdom, geodes are called **"potato stones."**

- The geode is the state rock of **Iowa**.

- It is illegal to remove geodes from **state parks**.

- When crystals fill the interior of a cavity completely, it is called a **thunderegg** rather than a geode.

- The **Crystal Cave**, located in Put-in-Bay, Ohio, is said to be the largest geode in the world.

- It has been said if you whisper your **heart's desire** into an open geode it will come true.